New Vanguard • 3

Sherman Medium Tank 1942–45

Steven J Zaloga • Illustrated by Peter Sarson

First published in Great Britain in 1993 by
Osprey Publishing, Midland House,
West Way, Botley, Oxford OX2 0PH, UK
44-02 23rd St, Suite 219, Long Island City, NY 11101, USA
Email: info@ospreypublishing.com

ISBN 978 1 85532 296 7

CIP Data for this publication is available
from the British Library
Filmset in Great Britain
Printed in China through World Print Ltd.

10 11 12 13 14 27 26 25 24 23 22 21 20 19 18

FOR A CATALOGUE OF ALL BOOKS PUBLISHED BY
OSPREY MILITARY AND AVIATION PLEASE CONTACT:

Osprey Direct, c/o Random House Distribution Center,
400 Hahn Road, Westminster, MD 21157
Email: uscustomerservice@ospreypublishing.com

Osprey Direct, The Book Service Ltd, Distribution Centre,
Colchester Road, Frating Green,
Colchester, Essex, CO7 7DW
Email: customerservice@ospreypublishing.com

www.ospreypublishing.com

Acknowledgements
The author would like to thank the staffs of the US Army
Institute for Military History, Carlisle Barracks; the Patton
Museum, Ft. Knox; the National Archives, Washington DC;
the Federal Record Center, Suitland MD; and the Marine
Historical Division. The author would like to express his
special gratitude to Col. James Leach, formerly of 37th Tank
Battalion, 4th Armored Division; to 'Sliver' LaPine, 8th
Tank Battalion; and to Col. Henry Gardiner, Frank Clay,
Alvin Parham and John Elliot, all of 13th Armored Regiment
(13th Tank Battalion), 1st Armored Division, for their patient
answers to my many questions.

Author's Note
For those seeking a more thorough technical study of
the Sherman the author highly recommends *Sherman -
A History of the US Medium Tank,* by R. Hunnicutt.
The evaluations of the Sherman contained here are based on
interviews with former Sherman crewmen; on wartime
interviews with Sherman crews conducted by US Army
Intelligence and other branches of the service; and on
Ordnance Department evaluations. The material quoted from
crews of the 2nd Armored Division is taken from a special
report prepared for Gen. Eisenhower in 1945 on the
inadequacies of the Sherman in combat. All photos are from
the US Army, unless otherwise indicated.

DESIGN AND DEVELOPMENT

The development of American tanks, in the engineering sense, was undertaken by the Ordnance Department. However, Ordnance was limited to initiating design studies unless a formal requirement was issued by the user service, in this case the Armored Force, and production decisions required the approval of Army Ground Forces (AGF) headed by Maj. Gen. Lesley McNair. The AGF was responsible for formulating Army tactical doctrine, and came heavily to reflect the opinions and biases of McNair, an artilleryman with prodigious administrative skills but no combat experience. McNair felt that tanks had no business jousting with other tanks, and that this task should be left to his pet service, the Tank Destroyers. Tanks were envisaged as infantry support weapons (in the case of those belonging to independent tank battalions) or as tools for rapid 'cavalry' exploitation of breakthroughs in the case of those of the armoured divisions. The breakthrough would be secured by the infantry divisions with local support from the independent tank battalions to soften up particularly tenacious defensive positions, and any sallies by enemy tanks would be greeted by towed or self-propelled tank destroyers. With a gap secured, the armoured divisions would pour through to wreak havoc in the enemy rear, destroying reinforcements, disrupting the command structure and forcing the enemy infantry to flee or be destroyed. This American approach was in distinct contrast to German doctrine, which viewed the Panzer divisions as a vital mass of mobile firepower, central to the securing of the breakthrough against both armoured and unarmoured opposition, as well as to the rapid exploitation of success.

The basic fallacy of the American doctrine was the inability of the tank destroyers to deal

Crew of an M3 Lee of 'E' Co., 2nd Medium Tank Battalion 13th Armoured Regiment, US 1st Armored Division pose beside their tank at Souk-el-Arba, *Tunisia, on 26 November 1942. The M3 was the precursor of the Sherman and, though obsolete, was used extensively in the fighting in North Africa.*

completely with enemy armour. The McNair doctrine presumed a certain amount of concentration of German armour, since a single tank destroyer battalion could hardly be expected adequately to cover an entire divisional front. But with Allied air superiority, concentration of armour by the Germans became extremely risky except on a small scale for local counter-attacks. Tanks were, inevitably, obliged to deal with German tanks, usually without tank destroyer support. Moreover, the tank destroyers were not particularly useful armoured vehicles. They were essentially under-armoured tanks with slightly bigger guns, and could not slug it out on even terms with their heavily-protected German adversaries. Since they were open-topped they were very vulnerable to overhead airbursts, mortar fire and even dedicated infantry attack. They were adequate weapons for ambush or fire support; but since the 1944–45 campaign was a string of unbridled offensive drives, they did not fulfil the needs of the US Army. As a First Army report bitterly complained, what was needed was not tank killers, but killer tanks.

Lt.Col. Henry Gardiner stands before his M4A1 Sherman 'Henry III'. Gardiner's previous two tanks were knocked out in earlier fighting in Tunisia, and this particular vehicle was destroyed by a German anti-tank gun near Mateur with the loss of two crewmen. The geometric insignia identifies this vehicle as being with the HQ Co., 2nd Medium Tank Battalion, 13th Armoured Regiment, 1st Armoured Division. Col. Gardiner went on to command the 13th Tank Battalion in Italy, but named his subsequent tank 'Ballykinler'. (Henry E. Gardiner)

The Ordnance search for the killer tank was stymied by the smug complacency of the AGF, and by a major failure in the Army as a whole to appreciate the growing shift within the Wehrmacht towards even heavier and better-armed tanks. The Sherman had proved capable of dealing with the PzKpfw III and IV on equal terms, but its hopeless showing against the Tiger was brushed aside by unfairly blaming the heavy losses at Faid Pass on the inexperience of the troops, and by assuming that the Tiger would be encountered in small numbers and could therefore be dealt with by artillery or tank destroyers. These attitudes were summed up in an AGF policy statement to the Chief of Staff in November 1943 opposing the production of the excellent new T26 (M26 Pershing) heavy tank:

'The recommendation of a limited proportion of tanks carrying a 90mm gun is not concurred in for the following reasons: The M4 tank has been hailed widely as the best tank on the battlefield today. There are indications even the enemy concurs in this view. Apparently, the M4 is an ideal combination of mobility, dependability, speed, protection and firepower. Other than this particular request– which represents the British view–there has been no call from any theatre for a 90mm tank gun. There appears to be no fear on the part of our forces of the German Mark VI (Tiger) tank There can be no basis for the T26 tank other than the conception of a tank-vs-tank duel – which is believed to be unsound and unnecessary. Both British and American battle experience has demonstrated that the anti-tank gun in suitable numbers and disposed properly is the master of the tank… There has been no indication that the 76mm anti-tank gun is inadequate against the German Mark VI tank.'

The contemptuous view of British opinion on this subject was widely shared in the US, and stemmed from the abysmal quality of British tank design in the early years of the war. Yet the combat-wise British liaison officers appreciated what their American counterparts had failed to understand through their own inexperience – that German tank design was not stagnant. Driven by the need to surpass excellent Soviet tank designs like the T-34, there was a constant escalation of German armour and firepower. The British had witnessed the leap from the 20mm and 37mm guns of 1940, to the 50mm and short 75mm in 1941, and finally to the long 75mm of the PzKpfw IV Special (Ausf.F) and the 88mm of the Tiger in Tunisia in 1943. The same improvements had taken place in tank armour as well. The British had every expectation that they would face an even more dangerous adversary in France in 1944, and saw their fears borne out when liaison teams in Moscow reported in July 1943 that the Russians had captured a new 45-ton medium tank called the Panther, with excellent sloped armour and a potent new long-barrelled 75mm gun. To deal with this threat the British had developed a special mounting for the excellent 17pdr. antitank gun that could be crammed even into the small turret of the 75mm gun Sherman. This fine weapon was offered to the Ordnance Dept. in the autumn of 1943, and was ignored. The Sherman with 17pdr. gun, called the Firefly, was issued to British and Commonwealth tank troops initially on the basis of one vehicle per troop, to deal more effectively with the new German tanks. The American tankers would not be so lucky.

Part of the resistance within the US Army to a heavy tank like the T26 to supplement the Sherman was a legitimate concern over logistics. American tanks had to be shipped thousands of miles to distant battlefields in Europe and the Pacific, and every extra ton of tank was a ton less of other vital supplies. The T26 weighed nearly 50 per cent more than the Sherman and would require elaborate new training, new spare parts and new ammunition. The Army was not convinced of the need for this tank, anyway. To some extent this concern over logistics was exaggerated. The Soviet Union, whose heavy industries were stretched far more thinly than those of the US, managed to provide the Soviet Army with excellent heavy tanks throughout the war without insuperable logistics problems. As a compromise, the AGF agreed to up-arm the M10 tank destroyer with the T26's 90mm gun, resulting in the M36; and agreed to allow the limited production of up-armed Shermans with a 76mm gun which Ordnance had been

pushing since 1942. The 76mm gun was chosen rather than a different and more potent weapon since it fired the same ammunition already in use by the M10 and M18 tank destroyers. It was a short-sighted move, as this gun was barely capable of defeating existing German tanks like the Tiger I, and provided no leeway for newer tanks with even better armour. This development was greeted with ambivalence by the Armored Force. While a better tank gun was desired, the M1A1 76mm gun chosen was only marginally better than the 75mm gun in anti-tank performance, while lacking the advantage of the 75mm gun's excellent HE round

'Condor', an M4A2 of 'C' Co., 2nd Marine Tank Bn., was one of a handful of Shermans successfully landed on Tarawa on 'D-Day', 20 November 1943, marking the operational debut of the M4 in the Pacific. 'Condor's' combat career was shortlived as it was inadvertently bombed by a US Navy plane which had not been informed that there were Marine tanks ashore, and presumed it to be Japanese. The elephant insignia was the marking of the 2nd Marine Tank Battalion (USMC)

for general support. On this subject, the Armored Force summarised its position in September 1943:

'The 76mm gun M1 as a tank weapon has only one superior characteristic to the 75mm gun M3. This superior characteristic is in armour penetrating power. The 76mm gun will penetrate on an average of one inch more armour than the 75mm gun M3 at the same range. The high explosive pitching power of the 76mm gun is inferior to the 75mm gun. The 76mm HE shell weighs 12.37lb and has a charge of .86lb explosive. The 75mm HE shell weighs 14.6lb and has a charge of 1.47lb explosive. The exterior ballistics of the 76mm gun are generally less satisfactory for a general purpose Medium Tank weapon than the 75mm gun. The 76mm gun has an extremely heavy muzzle blast, such that the rate of fire when the ground is dry is controlled by the muzzle blast

dust cloud. Under many conditions this dust cloud does not clear for some eight to thirty seconds. The presence of this heavy muzzle blast makes the sensing of the round extremely difficult for the tank commander and gunner... The characteristics of the complete round of the 76mm gun makes it possible to stow only approximately 70 per cent as many rounds of ammunition in the Medium Tank M4 for the 76mm gun as can be stowed for the 75mm gun M3. The great length of the 76mm round slows the loader and somewhat slows the rate of fire... If the 76mm gun as adopted for all Medium Tanks in a division then insofar as the attack of all targets except enemy armor is concerned a handicap has been imposed on the Medium Tank... It is believed that a fairly good percentage of 76mm guns should be included in a Medium Tank unit for the purpose of giving it a sufficient share of the additional penetrating power obtainable with the 76mm gun.'

The Armored Force recommended that about one-third of the Shermans be armed with the 76mm gun, but none were available for the armoured divisions until after the landings in Normandy.

Tanks of 'E' Co., 66th or 67th Armd. Regt., 2nd Armd. Div. advance along a hedgerow near Champ du Bouet, France during the bocage fighting in Normandy, 10 August 1944. The lead tank, an M4A1(76mm)W, *was among the original batch of new 76mm gun tanks to arrive in France. Although originally scorned, the 76mm gun tanks were much sought-after following the first encounters with Panthers.*

That the Sherman was so successful is all the more surprising given such barren roots. Tank development in the US in the 1940 languished under the restrictions of a parsimonious Congress and an antiquated tactical doctrine that were not overcome until the staggering defeat of France in 1940. Production and design facilities in the US were hardly more elaborate than those of a small European state like Sweden or Poland, yet Roosevelt's commitments to Britain in 1940 necessitated rapid expansion to production levels in excess of those of the major European powers. In the summer of 1940 the US Army was about to adopt the M2A1 medium tank, a pathetic symbol of the depths to which Ordnance Department designs had sunk, armed with a tinkertoy assortment of machine guns and a single paltry 37mm tank gun. Reassessments

forced on the Army by the French defeat made it horribly clear that the planned production of 1000 M2A1s would be foolish in the extreme.

Fortunately the Army could depend on a vigorous and mature steel industry and some of the best automotive and locomotive factories in the world. While the redesign of the M2A1 was undertaken, plans were laid for quantity tank production. It was evident that it would be at least a year before casting facilities would be ready to handle turrets capable of mounting a 75mm gun, so a stop-gap design was completed carrying a 75mm gun in a sponson mount, and a 37mm gun in a small turret, in much the same configuration as the French Char B1 tank. This began to roll of the assembly lines in June 1941 as the M3 medium tank. It formed the backbone of the newly-formed armoured divisions, and was supplied to British tank units fighting in the Western Desert through Lend-Lease. Although well-accepted by its British crews, the peculiar gun arrangement and the resultant excessive vehicle height doomed the M3 to a short production life of only 15 months; some 4,924 were built and saw combat service in the American, British, Soviet and some Commonwealth armies.

Using virtually the same chassis and power train as the M3 medium, the new M4 was designed around a large cast turret capable of mounting an M3 75mm tank gun. The initial production model,

To help break out of the hedgerows Shermans were fitted with the so-called Cullin Devices, better known as 'Rhinos', which consisted of old 'Rommel Asparagus' beach obstructions cut up to make prongs. This helped the Sherman to dig into the hedge and crash through it without

'porpoising' and exposing the thinner belly armour. This M4A1 of the 741st Tank Bn. is fairly remarkable in that it was still fitted with the 'Rhino' on 9 March 1945. Most of these prongs were dropped immediately after the conclusion of Operation 'Cobra'.

the M4A1, used a cast-armour hull, and first rolled off the assembly lines in February 1942. Since there were not enough casting facilities to provide hulls in the quantities anticipated, the M4 welded-hull version was developed, and became available in July 1942. In 1942 the initial US Army plans called for 60 armoured divisions, and Roosevelt announced a suitably ambitious production programme for 45,000 tanks in that year alone. This would have entailed manufacturing as many tanks every four days as had been manufactured in the US in the previous ten years! Clearly a major stumbling-block was going to be engine production. The M4 and

M4A1 were both powered by the Wright-Continental R-975 Whirlwind radial aircraft engine, which unfortunately was also in demand by the Navy and Army Air Force. To supplement these, Ordnance decided to adopt the GM Twin 6-71 diesel, which consisted of a pair of bus engines joined at the flywheel end by a clutch and transfer unit. Although the new Armoured Force entertained the notion of using exclusively diesel engines in all its tanks, this idea was dropped in 1942 when Quartermaster Corps complained about the logistic difficulties of supplying armoured units with both diesel fuel for tanks and petrol for motor transport.

The diesel-powered M4, designated M4A2, became available in April 1942 and was earmarked for Lend-Lease. The only significant combat use of the M4A2 by American forces was its employment in Marine tank battalions; diesel-powered tanks were preferred by the Navy since they used the same fuel as small craft. The Ford GAA engine was also adopted in 1942, with the first of these M4A3 tanks being manufactured in June 1942. Although not produced in the quantities of the M4 or M4A1, it was the preferred variant of the US Army. The final engine type developed for the M4 was the Chrysler A-57 multi-bank which consisted of four automobile engines mated together; it was so long that it required a lengthened hull, and was manufactured as the M4A4, almost exclusively for the British forces although there was some US training use. Regardless of the enormous production capacity of American heavy industry, the drain on steel production by the shipbuilding industry whittled down the President's ambitious tank production programme to more manageable levels.

VARIANTS

The principal types of Shermans in US Army service in 1944 were the M4 and the M4A1. They were identical internally, both being powered by the Continental Whirlwind radial engine, but the M4 had a welded hull and the M4A1 a cast armour hull. Some units preferred the M4A1, feeling that the rounded surfaces warded off enemy projectiles better; but in at least one tank

An M4A1 Duplex Drive (DD) Sherman of the 756th Tank Bn. supporting troops of the 1st Inf. Regt. at Alpha Yellow Beach (Pampelonne) on 15 August 1944 during the invasion of southern France. The DD tank was a regular Sherman with an erectable flotation device designed to enable it to swim ashore from landing craft. They were used with mixed results during the Normandy landings by three US tank battalions, and were also used by American forces during the Rhine crossings.

battalion, the 73rd, the troops became convinced that the cast armour was inferior to that on the M4, and avoided using M4A1s in combat. Most units could see no difference between the two types, though the welded hull version did have a bit more interior. space. By August 1944 more M4A3s were becoming available, and the troops soon took a liking to them because of the greater horsepower, greater torque at low speeds and better reliability of the engine. Otherwise, the M4A3 was very similar in appearance to the M4 except for the engine grille-work and a different air-filter configuration at the rear.

The layout of the Sherman was conventional. The engine was mounted in the rear behind a firewall, and the power train passed under the turret basket to the clutch and transmission in the front of the tank. Due to the use of a radial engine in the initial Shermans the powertrain was mounted quite high in the hull, resulting in a tall silhouette for the tank. This made the Sherman a more conspicuous target, but on the positive side it provided more interior space, allowing more ammunition to be stored than in most tanks of its day. The crew consisted of five men: the driver in the left hull front, the assistant driver/bow machine gunner beside him in the right hull front, and a turret crew of three the tank commander in the right-rear of the turret, the gunner immediately in front of him, and the gun loader in the left side of the turret.

Firepower

The Sherman was armed with an M3 75mm gun fitted with a gyro-stabiliser for one axis (elevation) stabilisation. The standard anti-tank round was the M61 APC, which could penetrate 68mm of armour at 500 metres and 60mm at 1000m. The round weighed 20lb of which the projectile was 15lb. The other standard rounds were the M89 White Phosphorus (WP 'Willy Peter') Smoke and the M48 High Explosive. The maximum theoretical rate of fire was 20 rounds per minute, though this was seldom attempted or achieved in combat.

The turret was traversed from the gunner's or commander's position by a hydraulic and electric unit, and the gunner had a manual traverse wheel as well. The Sherman had a very fast turret traverse for its day, which was one of the few advantages it possessed over the Panther. In the early Shermans the gunner had a periscopic sight for aiming the main gun, but this proved troublesome as the articulated linkage easily misaligned. A telescopic sight was developed and fielded in 1943. Tanks fitted with the M70 telescopic sight were conspicuous by their use of the wider M34A1 gun mantlet. This was a three-power sight without special filters, and was good out to 1000m even though it did not have either the optical quality or the power of

A pair of M4s await further orders in the battered town of Coutances, 31 July 1944. The lead tank is armed with a 75mm gun, while the second vehicle mounts a 105mm howitzer These 105mm assault tanks were used by the HQ companies in tank battalions. The white stars have been overpainted on these tanks, as they provided a conspicuous target for German anti-tank gunners.

German sights, and could prove difficult to use if facing into the sun. Ranging was done by the commander or gunner by estimation using ballistic reticules in the sights. The 75mm Sherman was one of the first tanks fitted with a gyro-stabilised gun. Opinions on the value of this feature vary, with most veterans claiming it was worthless and was generally left turned off. It was not fitted in some 76mm tanks. Some tankers who had better luck with it insist that it was rarely used because it took care to keep in adjustment and thorough training to use properly, and most troops did not want to bother with either. As a result, most firing was done from a halt. The M3 75mm gun was flanked by a Browning .30 cal. machine gun. Firing of the main gun was by foot pedal or a button on the turret traverse handle.

Behind the gunner was the commander. In most 75mm Shermans the commander had a two piece split hatch immediately above him fitted with a single traversible periscope. There was a small vane sight in front of this periscope, and another located forward of the gunner's periscope.

M4A4 Shermans marshal in the fields outside Caen in early August 1944 in preparation for Operation 'Totalize'. Belonging to 1 Dywizja Pancerna, these Polish Shermans would later fight in the battles around Mont Ormel which closed the Falaise Pocket trapping much of the Wehrmacht in western France. (Sikorski Institute)

These two vanes could be aligned by the commander to 'rough-aim' the gun. They were later replaced by a single 'U'-shaped sight which was easier to use. The commander had very limited sighting from this periscope, and when the 76mm gun was introduced in the new T23 turret an improved commander's cupola was added which had all-round vision blocks giving a much more satisfactory view. Some late production 75mm gun tanks were also fitted with this feature. The commander talked to his crew through a small hand-held microphone. The tank's radio receiver was carried behind the commander in the rear turret bustle, and command tanks had an additional transmitter. Initially three out of five tanks had a receiver only, but by late 1944 the whole platoon usually had receivers and transmitters.

An all too common sight in the drive across France: in the Distance, a Sherman burns while a medic races to aid the wounded crew. In the foreground, a medic waits by the side of a crewman wounded when his tank was hit. Bayon, France 12 September 1944.

The loader sat or stood in the left side of the turret. The turret had brackets for 12 rounds of ammunition around the lower turret basket wall, and there were eight more rounds in a ready-rack under the gun. Originally the turret basket was heavily shielded by protective screening around most of the lower sides, but this was gradually reduced since it interfered with passing ammunition up from the stowage bins in the hull. There was a stowage rack for 15 rounds in the left sponson at the loader's knee, and racks for 15 and 17 rounds in the right sponson accessible to the commander. The main 30-round compartment was located under the turret basket behind the bow-gunner. This was awkward for him to reach, though the practice in some units was for the bow gunner to move his seat back, swing around backwards, and pass the rounds up through gaps in the turret basket wall. The main bin was a constant source of

complaints since it was very hard on the hands unless an 'ammunition puller' tool was used. As this was often misplaced, a screwdriver became a popular tool for prying the rounds out. Some crews became frustrated and tore out the bin's innards, simply stacking the ammunition like a pile of logs in the cardboard packing tubes it came in. The belly escape hatch was located in front of this bin. Strangely, in some areas this escape hatch became a prized item among local infantry units, who stole them to provide armoured overhead cover for their foxholes! This led to modification orders for chains to be added to prevent such thefts after some divisional commanders complained that they had tanks out of service missing this part.

There never seemed to be enough space for ammunition in the Sherman. It was common practice in most units to store additional rounds in every nook and cranny. In some cases this was the result of crew anxieties that they would not be adequately re supplied, but in some divisions in Patton's Third Army it was policy. American tank tactics in France stressed 'reconnaissance by fire' (that is, attacking likely targets where antitank guns or Panzerfaust teams might be lurking), the feeling being that it was cheaper in men and tanks to squander ammunition than to risk surprise attacks. Many a French church belfry fell victim to 'prophylactic fire'.

Probably the worst aspect of the loader's position was that he had no escape hatch and had to crawl under the gun to exit through the main (commander's) turret hatch. This led to a higher casualty toll among loaders than there need have been. Eventually a small oval hatch was added above the loader's position, though in the interim some units modified the protective guard around the back of the gun with hinges so that it could be swung out of the way to speed the loader's exit.

A typical firing sequence went as follows:

Commander to driver: 'Driver...STOP'
Commander to gunner: 'Gunner...TANK'
Commander to loader: 'AP'
Commander to gunner: 'Traverse left...
Steady-on...One thousand'
Gunner to Commander: 'Ready!'
Commander to gunner: 'FIRE!'

Besides the main gun, the Sherman had a coaxial .30 cal. Browning machine gun used to shoot-up enemy vehicles or infantry, and there was another in the right hull front in a ball mount operated by

The crew of an M4 of 37th Tank Bn., 4th Armd. Div., commanded by Sgt. T. Dunn, prepare to bed down for the night after a lull in the fighting near Chateau *Salinas, 26 September 1944. This particular tank has the wider M34A1 mantlet that permitted the use of a new telescopic aiming-sight for the main gun.*

A column of M4A2 Shermans of 4 Pulk Pancerny, 2 Brygada Pancerna in training before their combat initiation at Monte Cassino. This Polish unit was raised in Palestine, hence its desert paint scheme of Light Mud and Blue-Black. It carries the Polish regimental insignia, a scorpion, on the turret front. (Sikorski Institute)

the bow-gunner. It was a reliable weapon, if a bit hard to change barrels. On the commander's cupola was a .50 cal. Browning, ostensibly placed there for anti-aircraft fire, but more often used to reach out to targets beyond the range of the .30 cal. Brownings. It was rather awkwardly placed, obliging the commander to expose himself to aim it properly, but it was a very destructive weapon against targets such as trucks or wooden buildings. When not in use it was stowed in clips on the rear of the turret with the barrel removed.

The 75mm gun tanks began to be supplemented by the newer 76mm gun tanks in July 1944. They made up as much as one-third of some battalions, and by 1945 some battalions had nearly half their complement armed with 76mm guns. The new vehicles, first the M4A1(76mm)W and later the M4A3(76mm)W were easily identifiable by the new, larger T23 turret and the long barrel of the gun. There were other less apparent changes such as the larger driver/bow-gunner hatches, and the one-piece 47° hull front on the M4A3. Internally, the vehicles had 'wet stowage'– see below.

The M1A1C 76mm gun fired the same ammunition as the M10 and M18 tank destroyers. There were two rounds commonly available for it: the M42A1 HE weighing in at 22.6lb, and the M62 APC-T round which weighed 25lb with a 15.5lb projectile. Less common, and in great demand, was the T4 HVAP-T round weighing 19lb with a 9.4lb projectile. Called 'souped up AP' or 'hyper-shot', this tungsten-cored round was always in short supply in tank battalions as it was reserved for tank destroyers. Seldom were there more than two or three rounds available for each 76mm gun tank before 1945, when a lucky outfit might have as many as five. It was saved for dealing with Panthers and Tigers. At 500m the standard APC round could punch through 98mm of armour, compared to about 150mm for HVAP, and at 1000m it was 90mm against 132mm.

Some Shermans had a small single-fire smoke mortar mounted in the turret. Opinions on this device vary; some units did not use them, as they found that when they were fired to provide cover the Germans tended to spray the smoke cloud with machine gun fire, much to the consternation of infantry accompanying the tank. The WP smoke round was a preferred means of concealment in many units, even though considered too small and slow.

Protection

The hull armour on the Sherman was 51mm thick in front and 38mm on the sides. The turret had an 89mm gun shield, and the turret armour ranged from 76mm at the front to 51mm on the side. On the late production welded-hull models the armour was raised to 63mm on the hull front. The Sherman's armour could be penetrated at most ordinary combat ranges by any of the tanks and self-propelled guns commonly in Wehrmacht service in 1944, with the minor exception of older types like the PzKpfw III, which were infrequently encountered. For example, the PzKpfw IV Ausf. H, which was one of the more common types in service, could penetrate the frontal armour with AP rounds from ranges in excess of 2000m, or the sides from over 4500m. The Sherman had been designed to resist the old 37mm PAK 36 which the Germans had started to replace in 1940 after the fall of France. The chassis could not accept too much more armour without sacrificing mechanical reliability, and so this was not seriously considered. This situation was very demoralising to American tank crews in Europe, since their tanks were regularly knocked out by everything from hand-held Panzerfausts to 88mm anti-aircraft guns, while they watched with utter disgust as the shells from their own guns bounced harmlessly off Panthers and Tigers.

The Sherman, besides being thinly armoured, also had the reputation of a fire-trap. This was popularly attributed by many in the US Army to the decision to use petrol engines rather than diesels. This view was sparked by the Tank Destroyer command's pitch to its troops about the supposed advantages of the diesel engines (used in

some of the M10s) over the petrol engines used in most US Army Shermans. A popular initiation rite for new troops in these TD units was to order them to the engine deck of a diesel M10 and tell them to determine how full the fuel tank was.

When the 'rube' admitted being unable to see anything in the dark interior of the fuel tank, his tormentor would strike a match and hurl it into the open pipe. Not being familiar with diesel fuel, the 'rube' would assume that the match was about to ignite a major conflagration and would hurl himself to the ground in a most unseemly fashion, much to the delight of previously initiated onlookers.

In fact, battlefield experience and Ordnance tests established that the main cause of Sherman fires was ignition of the ammunition propellant. A lesser culprit was the occasional ignition of turret hydraulic oil, personal stowage or sometimes fuel. It was estimated that 60-80 per cent of Shermans

New M4A3(76mm)W tanks of the 2nd Platoon, 'A' Co., 13th Tank Bn., 1st Armd. Div., fire their guns near Lorenzana, Italy, on 19 August 1944. The red barrel bands indicated 'A' Co., while the presence of two stripes on the gun tube and the number '2' to the rear of the turret sides indicated 2nd Platoon The second tank, with its half-barrel band, is the vehicle of the company commander.

Mines are always a constant threat to tanks, and this danger led to bizarre counter-measures. Here a T1E3 of the 738th Tank Bn (Special) prepares to clear a stretch of road near Beggendorf, Germany, on ll December *1944. About 200 of these 'Aunt Jemima' mine-rollers were built; while effective on roads, they were less popular with the troops than the flail-type mine detonators as they easily bogged down on soft terrain.*

penetrated by AP rounds or Panzerfausts burned. This is easy to believe in view of the fact that a penetration from nearly anywhere in the frontal arc would bring a projectile in contact with ammunition, and once the casing ruptured, the HE filler used in many German AP rounds would ignite it. The common practice of storing 30 or 40 additional rounds of ammunition outside the bins and racks only served to exacerbate this problem. Once a propellant fire broke out the crew had little choice but to abandon the vehicle as quickly as possible.

Ordnance developed two solutions to this problem. As a short-term solution, plates of appliqué armour 25–35mm thick were added to the hull sides over the two right-hand ammo bins and one left-hand bin to lessen the chance of penetrations at these vulnerable spots. This was reasonably effective against the smaller calibre anti-tank weapons still encountered in Italy in 1943 and early 1944, but it was ineffective against hits by Panthers, Tigers or Panzerfausts.

In February 1944 some late production M4A3s had 'wet' stowage bins added: these consisted of racks surrounded by water. When the bins were hit by an AP round they poured water over the spilled propellant, either preventing a fire or inhibiting it long enough to allow the crew to escape. The propensity of American crews to pile in added ammunition meant that even this improvement could not be totally effective, but a study done by the Army in 1945 found that only 10–15per cent of the 'wet' stowage Shermans burned, as compared to 60-80 per cent of the 'dry' stowage Shermans. The wet stowage was used on M4A1s and M4A3s fitted with the 76mm gun, and on a small number of late M4A3s with the 75mm gun.

During the fighting in the bocage, where all travel was channelled down narrow tracks, Shermans became sitting ducks for concealed anti-tank guns. This led to some units using Shermans fitted with 'dozer blades as lead vehicles. The 'dozer blades were raised up, and sometimes sandbags were added for further cover. The practice was eventually discouraged since the added weight damaged the front bogie springs, and usually led to heat blistering on the front rubber wheels that could cause the solid rubber tyre to separate from the metal hub after 20 or 30 miles of driving on a hot summer day.

Ordnance had developed a more practical solution in the form of the M4A3E2 Jumbo assault tank. The Jumbo was an up-armoured M4A3 with extra plates 38mm thick added to the hull front and sides; a new 140mm-thick differential housing; and a new turret similar in appearance to the 76mm gun T23 turret, but 152mm instead of the 63mm of the standard production model. Only 254 were built, but they were very popular with the troops when they entered service in the autumn of 1944. The added weight led to decreased road speed, but the added protection more than compensated for this in the eyes of the troops. These tanks were used to lead columns down roads likely to be protected by concealed anti-tank guns. They were initially armed with 75mm guns but were subsequently retro-fitted with the 76mm, and some had hull flamethrowers added as

well. Production was curtailed when the decision was made to proceed with the production of the M26 Pershing heavy tank. Unfortunately, due to the AGF's previous foot-dragging, only a handful of M26s reached Europe before the end of the war, and so the Sherman continued to bear the full brunt of tank fighting long after it should have.

Following the climactic battles during the breakout from Normandy and the resultant annihilation of

'Annabelle', an M4A1 of Co. 'A', 48th Tank Bn., 14th Armd. Div., takeoff up firing position to launch a salvo of 4.5in. rockets from its 'Calliope' launcher. These T34 Calliope rocket launchers were effective area-saturation weapons, but were generally disliked by their crews, who often wondered what they were doing in the artillery business! On the original version the Main gun could not be fired unless the launcher aiming arm was removed, but on this vehicle the elevating arm has been welded to the mantlet to permit the use of the 75mm gun.

A close-up look at a PzKpfw V Ausf. G Panther hit by eight rounds of 76mm APC near Saverne, France. The gouges of six of these rounds are evident, only the hit on the lower left corner of the glacis plate causiug a minor penetration. The 76mm gun could only get penetrations against the front of the Panther by using the scarce HVAP ammunition, or by firing from a dangerously close range.

much of the Panzer force in the Falaise Pocket, German armoured vehicles were not again encountered in such large concentrations until the Ardennes counter-offensive. While German tanks were still met with frequency in small numbers, anti-tank rockets like the Panzerfaust and Panzerschreck became an increasing threat to the Sherman. These weapons were difficult to use effectively unless fired from very close ranges, but their shaped-charge warheads could easily penetrate the armour of a Sherman, and almost invariably started a fire. To provide some added protection against these sort of attacks American tankers began adding various sorts of improvised armour to their vehicles. In some units spare track links were draped over the front hull to provide some 'stand-off' protection. The most common approach was to add a layer of sandbags to the front, and sometimes even to the sides of the hull and turret. This was accomplished by welding an 'I' beam along the hull side to support the weight of the sandbags, then adding a frame of metal rod or thin girders to contain the sand bags. This load usually amounted to about 150 sandbags, which added two to three tons to the weight of the vehicle. Their effectiveness in stopping Panzerfausts was somewhat questionable, as is apparent from this account by a Sherman gunner of the 2nd Armored Division:

'We were attacking in a Sherman with 75mm gun. Visibility was very good. There were Jerries dug in about 40 yards in front of our tank in a line of foxholes. Several were flushed out and moving to the rear when a Jerry bazooka hit the left track and broke it. We were unable to back up when a second shot hit in front of the turret, but did not pierce the turret. The third hit the front of the tank, dislodging all the sandbags, about 40 in all, and cracked the front plate. The fourth hit the same spot and cracked the front slope still wider and set the tank on fire. The fifth shot hit the extra armor plate welded to the front plate of the bow gunner, about 1½ inches thick, and knocked that off and cracked the front plate.'

Even if only occassionally effective, the sandbag armour was a good morale booster for troops who were otherwise anxious about the indifferent quality of their equipment. Some units, such as 4th Armored Division, discouraged the use of sandbags because of their questionable ballistic value and the adverse effect they had on the weight and therefore the performance of the tank, preferring other methods instead. Besides using spare track shoes, the 4th Armored also cut the armour off disabled Panther tanks and welded it to the front of Shermans to provide additional improvised assault leaders like the E2 Jumbos.

The use of improvised armour was very widespread in the Pacific in the last year of the war, particularly on Marine tanks. The main threat to Marine Shermans were the Japanese anti-tank suicide teams which attacked with satchel-charges, shaped charges on pungi sticks, and magnetic anti-tank mines with shaped-charge warheads. The Marine 4th and 5th Tank Battalions built false sides on their Shermans with wood and sheet metal, about four inches out from the real hull sides. This provided enough 'stand-off' to diminish the effect of shaped-charge weapons. Those using sheet metal sides were usually painted with a sand mixture to make it more difficult to attach magnetic mines. The Japanese had a habit of placing satchel-charges on top of hatches, which were more vulnerable to explosive blast than the armour itself, so the Marines welded penny nails or steel grating over the hatches to provide several inches of 'stand-off' to dissipate the blast. Sandbags were added to other locations, particularly the rear engine deck, to prevent attachment of magnetic mines. All this added weight obliged the Marines to use duck-bill extenders on the track to prevent the tanks from sinking too deeply into the volcanic ash encountered on Iwo Jima.

Mobility

The Sherman was comparable to its contemporaries in mobility. It was capable of 25mph on a level road, and could be coaxed to 30mph if not over-

This interior view of an M4A3(76mm)W was taken from the commander's seat looking forward towards the gunner's position. The gunner's seat is folded down revealing the complex plumbing associated with the Oilgear hydraulic turret traverse mechanism. This particular vehicle has its telescopic and periscopic gunner's sights removed.

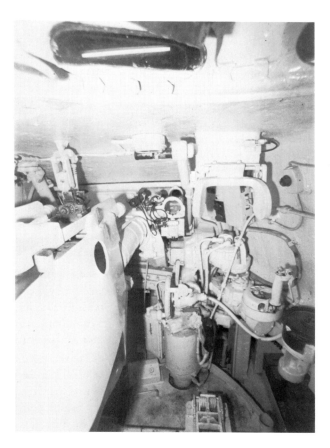

burdened with sandbags. Some crews tampered with the engine governors to squeeze a little more speed out of it, but this was discouraged as it often led to overstraining the engine. The Sherman performed best on dry terrain because of the narrow width of its track. On mud or snow it compared unfavourably with the later German tanks like the Panther or Tiger, which had been designed with very wide tracks as a result of experience on the Eastern Front. A Sherman driver from the 2nd Armored Division recalled:

'I saw where some Mk V [Panther] tanks crossed a muddy field without sinking the tracks over five inches, where we in the M4 started across the same field the same day and bogged down.'

Complaints of Shermans bogging down in sand in North Africa reached Ordnance in 1943, but there were two factors which inhibited satisfactory solutions. Army engineer regulations forbade vehicle widths beyond 124ins. due to shipping problems. A wider track would anyway have been difficult without a complete redesign of the suspension. As an expedient, in the spring of 1944, extended end connectors-better known to the troops as 'duck-bills'- were made available for attaching to the outer ends of the track. They reduced ground pressure from 14psi to 12psi, but were somewhat fragile and could easily be snapped off. Nonetheless, they were very necessary on overweight vehicles like the M4A3E2 Jumbos, or in very muddy conditions as prevailed in France and Italy in the autumn of 1944. The real solution was the development of new horizontal volute spring suspension (HVSS), which was introduced on the new M4A3E8 entering service in December 1944. Its wide track brought the ground pressure down to 11psi, which put US tanks on a more equal footing with their German adversaries.

Of the three major Sherman types used by the US Army the M4A3 was preferred because of its better engine. Both the M4 and M4A1 were rather underpowered and did not provide as much torque as might be desired at lower engine speeds. A frequent problem with the Whirlwind engine was that the spark plugs fouled excessively during extended idling periods, and the electrodes burned

An M4A2 of the French 2ᵉ Division Blindée passes through Strasbourg on 25 November 1944 on its way to the Rhine. The 2ᵉ DB was considered by the Americans to be the best of the French armoured divisions. The rather gaudy markings that adorned the tanks of the 'Division Leclerc' when they first landed in Normandy gradually became more restrained during the course of the fighting in northern France.

out on long road marches. This was hard to repair, as access to the lower bank of cylinders could frequently only be accomplished by removing the engine. The most vociferous critics of the Whirlwinds were the hapless crews who received reconditioned engines which had their cylinders chromed to replace worn surfaces. These were unreliable, had short lives and guzzled oil. The M4 and M4A1 were more prone to engine fires than the other Shermans due to the propensity of the Whirlwind to leak oil and petrol around the engine case and accessory mountings, and to blow oil out the crankcase breather, covering the cylinders and hot exhaust manifolds after piston rings had started to wear, and creating a blow-by. In spite of these problems, it should be kept in mind that compared to German or Soviet tank engines the Whirlwind was remarkably durable, and it compared rather badly only against other American tank engines.

Even though American tankers joked that the Ford GAA engine in the M4A3 'would be a real engine if it had a couple more cylinders', it was a more powerful engine than the Whirlwind and offered good torque at low engine speed. It was a bit of an oil-guzzler, and could be easily damaged by overspeeding. It took some getting used to after driving the M4 or M4A1 as it would spit or pop back if the throttle was opened too quickly at 500–800rpm, causing a momentary drop in power. It was more reliable and durable than the Whirlwind; and much as American tankers admired the Panther, the rapid drives across France and Germany would have been impossible in such a vehicle given its capricious engine performance.

OPERATIONAL HISTORY

The first unit to receive the M4A1 and M4 in any quantity was the 2nd Armored Division, which had been training on the M3 medium tank. In the summer of 1942 the division was obliged to divest itself of these tanks, which were shipped to North Africa for use by the British 8th Army in the forthcoming Alamein battles, where the M4 would see its combat debut. The 2nd Armored Division was subsequently re-equipped prior to its involvement in Operation 'Torch', the invasion of

A column of M4A3Ws of the 14th Armd. Div. passes by three Shermans disabled by mines near Barr, France, 29 November 1944. These particular vehicle are very late-production 75mm gun tanks with all-around vision cupolas and wet stowage. What appears to be a white sheet on the disabled tank to the right is in fact the cerise air identification panel commonly carried on American and British tanks to prevent Allied fighter-bombers from strafing them.

French North Africa. The 1st Armored Division was still equipped with the older M3 Lee[1] in most of its medium tank battalions when it sailed for North Africa. The first portion of the 1st Armored to arrive was Combat Command B (CCB), with two light battalions of M3 and M3A1 Stuarts and a medium battalion of M3 Lees. It was a cruel twist of fate that the better equipped 2nd Armored Division would see no major fighting after the initial amphibious landings, while the more poorly equipped battalions of the 1st Armored Division would see some of the most brutal combat of the Tunisian campaign while still manning obsolete tanks. The 2nd Bn., 13th Armd. Regt. became committed to the fighting in Tunisia soon after its M3 Lee tanks were landed. On 6 December 1942 a platoon of Shermans from the 66th Armd. Regt. (2nd Armd. Div.), sent into battle as reinforcements, was wiped out by concealed

AT guns during the disastrous fighting near Djebel bou Aoukar in an inauspicious combat debut of the M4 in American hands. Later in the month five platoons of Shermans from Cos. 'G' and 'H', 67th Armd. Regt. (2nd Armd. Div.) took part in the fighting around Long Stop Hill. The remainder of the 1st Armored Division arrived in Tunisia before Christmas, bringing with it the 2nd and 3rd Bns., 1st Armd. Regt. totally re-equipped with new M4A1s. These units were hurried to the Sidi bou Zid area, where a German counter-attack was expected. The German attack, named Operation 'Fruhlingswind', came crashing down through the Faid Pass, where the outnumbered 3rd Bn. 1st Armd. Regt. was nearly wiped out, losing 44 tanks. About 15 of these Shermans were knocked out by Tiger Is of sPzAbt. 501, which was in support of the main thrust by the 21st Panzer Division. An American counter-attack on 15 February suffered the same fate, with a loss of a further 40 Shermans, though some 19 PzKpfw IVs and 35 artillery pieces were knocked out. A badly emaciated 1st Armored Division took part in the subsequent Kasserine Pass fighting with what few Shermans and Lees remained. After being re-equipped with Shermans and crews from the 2nd Armored Division, a chastened but more experienced 1st Armored Division fought in the

[1] The British Army named American tanks in its service after American Civil War generals This was never officially accepted by the US Army, though some of the names were popular with the troops

An M4 105mm howitzer tank of the 48th Tank Bn., 14th Armd. Div. passes through Hochdelden, France, on 25 January 1945. The 105mm howitzer tanks were used by HQ companies to provide indirect and direct fire support for their battalions, and were used in *tank units instead of M7 'Priest' self propelled guns, which were too vulnerable due to their open tops. They are bedecked with a winter coat of lime and salt whitewash for camouflage, and the improvised sandbag armour is hardly noticeable on the front of the hull.*

final, successful offensives in Tunisia. It was a bloody battlefield initiation for the American armoured force, but it was a lesson taught by a master, and would not be forgotten.

The débâcle in Tunisia highlighted many command and organisational difficulties, which were corrected prior to the Sicily landing. It did not have any dramatic effect on armoured equipment. The Ordnance Department was already aware of the obsolescence of the M3 Lee, in spite of shameful attempts by Lt. Gen. Fredendall to try to hush up complaints from regimental commanders. The tankers were happy to get the new M4, which compared very favourably with the German PzKpfw IV in most respects, even if it could not take on the rare Tiger I on even terms. More disappointing was the performance of the M3 light tank, which was hopelessly undergunned for tank combat. A reorganisation of the armoured force improved this situation, but the inadequacies of the Stuart light tanks plagued American tankers through the remainder of the war.

The armoured division of 1942 was unwieldy and poorly balanced. It was intended for the exploitation of breakthroughs in a cavalry fashion rather than for assault and breakthrough like the Panzer divisions, and American field commanders felt it was tank-heavy and infantry-weak. There were two armoured regiments, each with three tank battalions, but only a single halftrack-borne armoured infantry regiment. The armoured regiments had two medium tank battalions and one light tank battalion. The September 1943 reorganisation changed this 'heavy' configuration to a 'light' configuration, with three tank battalions and three armoured infantry battalions. Due to the limited utility of the Stuart light tanks the new battalions were heterogeneous, having three companies of Shermans, and a single company of Stuarts for scouting and flank security. While the 1942 division had 232 M4s and 158 M5 light tanks, the 1943 division had 186 M4s and only 77 M5s. All of the 16 armoured divisions after 1943 followed the 'light' configuration except for the 2nd and 3rd Armored Divisions. Nearly all the independent tank battalions also followed the 1943 battalion configuration, and most light tank battalions were eventually re-equipped with Shermans.

American tank units taking part in Operation 'Husky', the invasion of Sicily, consisted of the 2nd Armd. Div., the 70th Light Tank Battalion (M5 Stuarts), and the 753rd Medium Tank Battalion (M4A1 Shermans). In the area around the Gela beachhead assaulted by the US 1st Infantry Division and 82nd Airborne Division was the Panzer Division 'Hermann Goring' supported by 17 Tigers of sPzAbt 504 and by R-35s of the Italian 131° Reggimento Carristi. The seasoned troops of the 'Big Red One' and the paras beat back the initial German tank attacks with ingenuity and guts, using captured Italian field guns, pack howitzers and bazookas. By the late afternoon of 11 July 1943, Shermans of the 753rd Tank Bn. arrived near Piano Lupo to support the 16th Infantry Regt., pushing back an

attack by sPzAbt 504 and knocking out three Tigers for a loss of four Shermans. Shermans of the 3rd Bn. 67th Armd. Regt., having extricated themselves from the soft sand and the entangling mess of Summerville matting on the beach, came to the support of the 18th Infantry and 41st Armd Inf.; they knocked out 15 PzKpfw IIIs and IVs The next morning a patrol of this unit Co 'G', 3/67th Armd. were forced to withdraw under artillery and air attack. In the process one Sherman was disabled. The remaining four Shermans stumbled into an ambush, losing one tank when it attempted to slug it out with a Tiger at 100 yards. However, when the German tanks made the mistake of passing by the disabled Sherman three were knocked out by flank shots.

By 16 July the German attacks on the beachhead had been decisively beaten, with the 'Hermann Goring' Division losing about 30 medium tanks, and 2./sPzAbt 504 losing 14 of its 17 Tigers. The 2nd Armored Division was scattered about in support of various paratroop and infantry regiments; when the rest of the division landed it was consolidated for a drive directed by its former commander, Lt.Gen. George S. Patton. Along with the 3rd Inf. Div., the 2nd Armored spearheaded a four-day, 100-mile drive on Palermo, capturing some 16,000 German and Italian prisoners and helping to erase some of the bitter memories of Tunisia.

Completely re-equipped with M4A1s and M5A1s, the 1st Armored Division was assigned to the Anzio landings. The division (minus CCB) sat out the frustrating stalemate that ensued, but played a major rôle in the breakout towards Rome on 12 May. There was much hard fighting, like that around Campoleone on 29 May where 21 Shermans were lost. But on 4 June 'Old Ironsides' rolled into Rome, the first Axis capital to fall to the Allies. The 1st was the only armoured division to remain in the Italian theatre for the rest of the war. Attention was soon shifting to another front.

The Sherman's painful début in the Mediterranean theatre was a prelude to the main encounter in France. Of the 16 armoured divisions and 65 independent tank battalions formed by the US Army in the Second World War, 15 of the armoured

Looking like a bit of rather tacky stage decor, this M4A3 105mm howitzer tank of the 751st Tank Bn photographed near Poretta, Italy, in February 1945 has been decorated with white paint and spun glass in a curious attempt at camouflage. The vehicle has been partly dug in at the rear to gain higher elevation for the howitzer. Due to the static nature of much of the fighting in Italy, tanks were more commonly used there in an indirect fire-support role.

divisions and 39 of the tank battalions fought in the European campaign of 1944–45. The heart of all these units was the Sherman tank; yet the Shermans present at Normandy were hardly different from the Shermans at Sidi bou Zid. While the Sherman was better than most German tanks encountered in North Africa and Sicily, with the obvious exception of the Tiger, by the time of the Normandy campaign it had fallen behind, particularly with the advent of the Panther tank.

Bocage and Breakout

The armoured divisions and tank battalions that landed in Normandy were equipped mostly with M4s and M4A1s, all with the 75mm M3 gun. In the second week of June a special demonstration of the new M4A1(76mm)W was held for Gen. Patton and several of the armoured division commanders who were about to enter combat in France. Though impressed, the divisional commanders did not want the new tank since none of their troops had trained on it yet. They relented when Patton agreed to accept some if they were confined to a separate battalion. What they still failed to understand was the difference in the Panzer divisions since Tunisia in 1943. The divisions encountered in Tunisia and on Sicily were equipped entirely with PzKpfw IIIs and PzKpfw IVs, that could be dealt with on equal terms by the Sherman. At Anzio in February 1944 the

1: M4A1, 'G'Co., 1st Armd.Regt., US 1st Armd.Div.,
   Sidi-bou-Zid, Tunisia, Feb.1943

2: M4Al, HQ Pltn., 'D'Co., 13th Tk.Bn., US 1st Armd.Div.,
   Italy, 1944

A

1: M4 command tank of Col. Creighton Abrams, 37th Tk.Bn., US 4th Armd.Div., France, 1944

2: M4, 3 Pltn., 'B'Co., 8th Tk.Bn., US 4th Armd.Div. Avranches, France, 1944

B

1: M4A2, 2^{e}Esc., 12^{e}Chasseurs d Afrique, 2^{e}DB,
   France, 1944

2: M4A2, 3^{e}Pltn., 4^{e}Esc., 2^{e}Cuirassiers, 1^{er}DB,
   Marseilles, France, 1944

C

M4A4 SHERMAN
75mm M3 gun, Chrysler A57 multibank engine

SPECIFICATIONS

Crew: 5
Combat weight: 34.8 tons
Power-to-weight ratio: 12.2 hp/ton
Hull length: 19 ft 10.5 ins.
Overall length: 19 ft 10.5 ins.
Width: 8ft 7 ins.
Engine: 425 hp Chrysler A57 multibank engine
Transmission: Synchromesh,
5 forward, 1 reverse
Fuel capacity: 160 gallons
Max. speed (road): 25 mph
Max. speed (cross-country): 20 mph

Best cruising speed: 38 kph
Max. range: 100 miles
Fuel consumption: 1.6 gallons per mile (cruising)
Fording depth: 42 ins. (without preparation)
Armament: 75mm M3 gun in M34 mount
Main gun ammunition: M61 APC (Armour-piercing)
M89 White Phosphorus
M48 High Explosive
Muzzle velocity: 2030 ft/sec (M61 APC)
Max. effective range: 14,000 yards
Stowed main gun rounds: 97
Gun depression/elevation: -12 degrees/ +8 degrees

KEY

1. Radio bracket
2. M3 75mm gun
3. Browning .30 cal machine gun
4. Co-driver/machine gunner's seat
5. Ventilator
6. Co-driver/machine gunner's hatch
7. Gyro stabiliser pump & motor
8. Main gun firing pedal
9. Ammunition stowage compartment
10. Turret basket
11. Oilgear hydraulic turret traverse mechanism
12. Browning .30 cal ammunition
13. Gyro-stabiliser control
14. Periscope
15. Indirect sighting device
16. Periscope
17. Browning .50 cal anti-aircraft machine gun mount
18. Ventilator
19. Commander's seat
20. M3 gun gyro-stabiliser
21. Co-axial Browning .30 cal machine gun
22. Periscope
23. Radio aerial
24. Fuel cut off
25. Synchromesh
26. Drive shaft
27. Transmission oil cooler
28. Chrysler A57 multibank engine
29. Fuel filler cap
30. Fire extinguisher
31. Air vent
32. Fuel tank
33. No.2 carburettor air cleaner
34. Auxiliary generator
35. Fire extinguisher
36. Generator
37. Parking brake
38. Gear selector
39. Driver's seat
40. Steering levers
41. Drive sprocket
42. Breather
43. Power train (final drive & brake system)
44. Towing ring

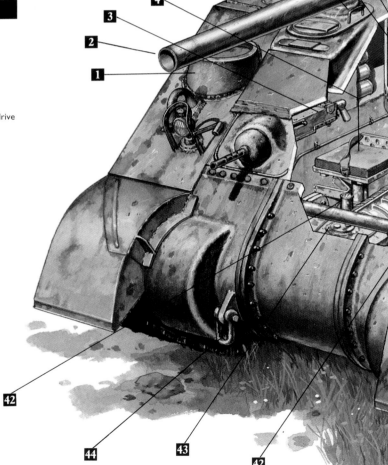

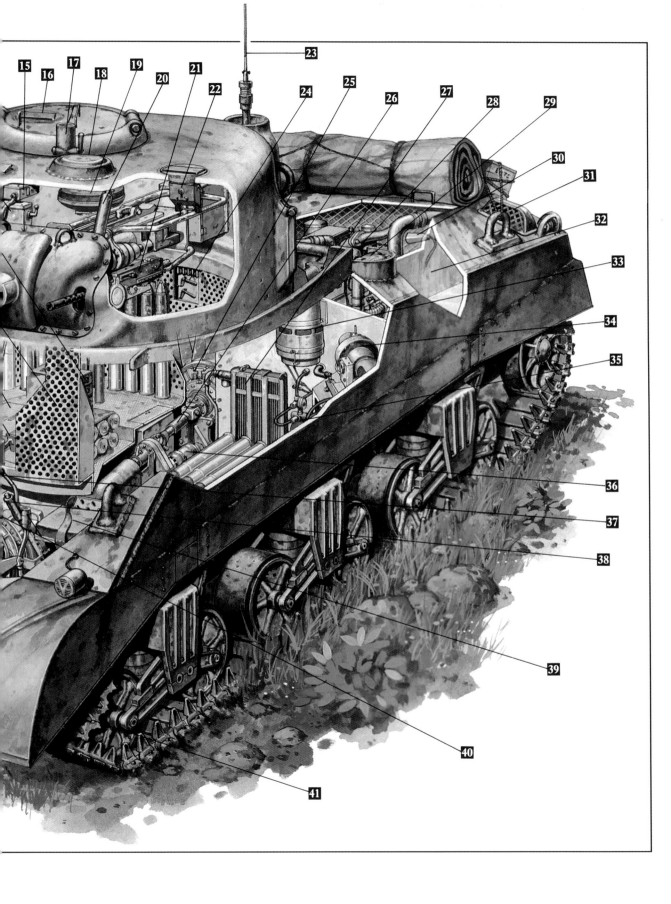

1: M4A1(76mm)W, Lt. T.Wialrowski. HQ 8qn.; 2 Pulk Pancerny,
   1 Dywizja Pancerna, Holland, 1944-45

2: M4A2, 2/Lt. M.Bialkiewicz, 2 Sqn., 4 Pulk Pancerny, 2 Brygada Pancerny, Cassino, Italy, 1944

E

1: M4A1, 3 Pltn., 'D' Co., US 2nd Armd.Div.,
Cotentin Peninsula, France, August, 1944

2: M4A3E8, 781st Tk.Bn., US 100th Inf.Div.,
Bitche, France, March 1945

F

1: M4A2(76mm)W, Soviet 9th Guards Tk.Bde., 1st Guards
Mech.Corps, Budapest, Hungary, 1945

2: M4A2(76mm)W, unidentified Soviet
tank brigade, Berlin, 1945

G

first Panthers began appearing in small numbers. In Tunisia the 1st Armored had faced only a single company of Tigers and the other Tiger company on Sicily had been mangled by infantry and paratroopers. However, of the 1608 Panzers in Normandy in the spring of 1944, 674 were late model PzKpfw IVs and 514 were Panthers. There were the equiva-

lent of more than three experienced full strength Tiger battalions in Normandy, though fortunately for the Americans they were mostly embroiled with the British near Caen. The frontal armour of the Panther could not be penetrated by the Sherman's 75mm gun at any range, though the Panther could easily knock out a Sherman from any practical range. One of the first encounters between Panthers and the 2nd Armored Division led to the report that a Sherman had been knocked out with the German 75mm round going through the transmission, through the ammunition rack on the hull floor, through the engine, and out the rear! After a few of these incidents there were no more reports of any reluctance to take the 76mm gun Shermans.

An M4A3(76mm)W clanks through the mud near Riedwihr, France, on 31 January 1945 in support of the 75th Inf. Div. during the destruction of the Colmar Pocket. This view clearly shows the large hatch added over the loader's station in the left of the turret on the 76mm gun version after complaints about the difficulty of the loader escaping when the tank was hit. The small square port on the turret side was used to dispose of spent shell casings.

A late production composite-hull M4 of the 44th Tank Bn. fire into a Japanese gun pit in the outskirts of Manila during the Philippines fighting, 10 March 1945. The composite-hull M4 had a cast front end and a conventional welded rear hull superstructure. This view shows the large air identification stars to good effect.

Indeed, there were howls of protest over the inadequacies of the Sherman, belated pressure to get the T26 into action as quickly as possible, and cries from tank battalions for new 'souped up' HVAP 76mm ammunition, which was the only type capable of regularly achieving frontal penetrations on the Panther.

It is hard to imagine worse tank country than the bocage of NW France. Protecting the fields from hard coastal winds, the age-old hedgerows were often too thick and high to be burst through by a tank, and were ideal defensive positions for German tank-killers lurking with Panzerfausts. In mid-July 3rd Armored Division was committed to the Cotentin fighting, following the 2nd Armored which had been in Brittany since the invasion. Initial skirmishes with the Panzer-Lehr Division

were marked by some success, since the Panther could not take advantage of its long-range firepower in the close terrain of the bocage. Operation 'Cobra', the breakout past St Lo, finally brought the US Army out into good tank country where its strong points became more evident – a reckless facility with mobile forces backed by a well-organised logistics train, formidable artillery and irresistible tactical air support. In spite of its shortcomings, the Sherman's mechanical durability would prove ideally suited to the explosive drive across France in the ensuing months of 1944.

Tank Combat

The Sherman could engage the PzKpfw IV with either the 75mm or 76mm gun at the usual battle ranges with a good prospect of success. Against the frontal armour of the Tiger, the 76mm gun firing APC could theoretically get penetrations against the front of the hull at ranges under 1200m, but the 75mm gun was incapable of penetrations of the frontal arc at any range. In theory, the 76mm could get frontal penetrations against the Panther firing

APC at ranges under 600m, but in fact this was seldom the case. The HVAP ammunition gave a much better probability of success. The fact that the 75mm could not get a frontal penetration on the Panther meant that Sherman units had to overwhelm these tanks by sheer numbers in order to manoeuvre towards the German's weaker flank, where the 75mm gun could successfully penetrate the armour. As Gen. Omar Bradley noted, 'this willingness to expend

The crew of 'Widow Maker', an M4A3 of 'C' Co., 4th Marine Tank Bn., take a breather during the fighting on Iwo Jima, 23 February 1945. It was not uncommon for a tank to have an official name, starting with the company letter, and an unofficial name as well. This view *clearly shows the modifications carried out by the Marines to protect their Shermans against Japanese suicide squads: spaced-out wooden side armour, spare track used for turret and front hull protection, rear hull sandbags, and wire grating over the hull and turret hatches. (USMC)*

Shermans offered little comfort to crews who were forced to expend themselves as well'. The patriotic baloney that the Sherman was the best tank in the world was widely bandied about in orientation speeches and in the press, and it was demoralising for the tank crews to listen to such nonsense after they had paid a high price to learn otherwise:

'On the morning of 20 November 1944 I was tank commander of a Sherman medium tank mounting a 76mm gun. The Germans staged a counter-attack with infantry supported by at least three Mark V [Panther] tanks. Ordering my gunner to fire at the closest tank, which was approximately 800 yards away, he placed one right in the side, which was completely visible to me. To my amazement and disgust, I watched the shell bounce off the side. My gunner fired at least six more rounds at the vehicle hitting it from the turret to the track... I was

completely surprised to see it moving after receiving seven hits from my gun.'

Sgt. F. W. Baker, 2nd Armd. Div.

'At Puffendorf, Germany, on 17 November 1944, my platoon of five M4 tanks were in a defensive position when the Germans launched a counter-attack with Mark VI [Tiger] tanks. My platoon was at that time composed of three 76mm guns and two 75mm guns. My own vehicle (75mm gun) was first to open fire on a Mark VI that was coming across the field towards us. We

M4A3(76mm)Ws of the 25th Tank Bn., 14th Armd. Div. take up firing positions outside Huttendorf, France, 11 February 1945. The lead tank still has sandbags on

the front hull, but they are missing from the side cage. The turret lacks sandbag protection and is camouflage-painted with thin, rolling stripes.

got a hit with the second round fired at 1300 yards, but from the tracer we could tell that the round ricochetted. At this time, several guns opened up… This concerted effort stopped the Tiger and prevented his advancing closer, but several direct hits from both types of guns obviously did not penetrate. This tank knocked out both my platoon sergeant's and my own vehicle, killing my driver and assistant driver and wounding me. The German tank eventually withdrew into defilade and presumably escaped across the Roer River'.

Capt. John Roller Jr. Co. 'A', 66th Armd. Regt., 2nd Armd. Div.

As more HVAP ammunition became available, the situation became more balanced:

'While on the right of the village of Fischeln, Germany…my position had a field of fire extending

Engineers put the finishing touches to a sandbag armouring job by painting the vehicle in Olive Drab and black swathes. When tanks carried so much extra weight, the 'duck-bill' extended end connectors were almost invariably fitted to give better floatation on soft soil. This particular tank belonged to 25th Tank Bn., 14th Armd. Div.

to a distance of 2000 yards covering several roads. While in this position, I spotted a Mark V moving across my front. My first shot I used an APC, establishing my range, which was 1600 yards. The next round was an HVAP. It hit the tank, immediately setting it on fire'.

Sgt. Ross Figueroa, 2nd Armd. Div.

After the Panther was first encountered in the Cotentin battles, tactics were developed to deal with the new menace where the Army bureaucracy had failed. To begin with, even when an American armoured division faced a Panzer division, the US units usually ended up with greater numbers of tanks since the Germans were invariably victims of attrition from tactical air strikes. By sheer numbers the Panthers could be overwhelmed if the US unit was willing to sacrifice a few Shermans keeping the Germans busy while other Shermans sought out the enemy's weak flank. Skilful tactics could reduce these casualties if the terrain was favourable. These tactics varied from unit to unit. Some units stressed getting off the first shot. While a shot that ricochetted harmlessly off the frontal armour would not unduly alarm an experienced Panther crew, a green or demoralised crew might lose heart and break off the engagement. A high explosive round might not disable a Panther or Tiger, but it could damage the sights, crack a track or jam a turret ring. The Achilles heel of the Panther was the shot-trap under the gun mantlet, and a well placed AP shot against the lower mantlet often deflected down against the thin roof armour above the driver, smashing into the hull ammunition pannier.

Col. James Leach, in 1944 a company commander with 37th Tank Bn., 4th Armored Division, recalled that in his unit at least one tank in each platoon was a 75mm gun tank. This was arranged because there was no WP smoke round for the 76mm gun. When venturing forward, the 75mm gun tank would keep a WP round loaded, and if an enemy

An M4A3E2 'Jumbo' (left) and M4A3E8 of the 37th Tank Bn., 4th Armd. Div. pass through Alzey, Germany, on 20 March 1945. The Sherman on the right is an HQ tank and is either Maj. Bautz's tank, 'Tornado', or Col. Creighton Abram's

'Thunderbolt'. (One of the earlier 'Thunderbolts' is shown in Plate B1.) The thick turret frontal armour on the Jumbo is very evident in this view. This particular assault tank has been re-armed with a 76mm gun; initially the Jumbos were armed with 75mm guns.

tank or SP gun was encountered that could not be dealt with frontally, it was attacked with the smoke round to prevent it from engaging the Shermans. Under favourable terrain conditions some of the Shermans could then scoot around and attack it from the sides or rear. In cases where this was not possible, air strikes or artillery were called in to loosen a tenacious defender.

Skill frequently overcame the Sherman's inadequacies. There were few better examples of this than the performance of Gen. 'P' Woods' superb

4th Armored Division at the battle for Arracourt. Following the gutting of the 112th Panzer Brigade by the Shermans of the French 2e Division Blindée and American P-47 fighter bombers, the Germans threw the XLVIII and LVIII Panzer Corps against the 4th Armored, which was spearheading US 3rd Army's drive across France. On 18 September 1944 Panthers of the 111th Panzer Brigade began the attack, but in two days of tough fighting they lost 43 tanks for only five Shermans and three M10 tank destroyers. The skirmishes east of Nancy by Col. Creighton Abrams' 37th Tank Bn. of CCA demonstrate Sherman tactics at their best.

On the evening of 18 September a force led by Major Hunter moved on Reichcourt. Capt. Spencer's Co. 'A', 37th Tank Bn. was to the north and Lt. James Leach's Co. 'B' was to the south, when around dusk Co. 'A' crested a ridge and encountered a laager of Panthers bedding down for the night. In a tactic Patton was wont to refer to as 'grabbing the

Kraut by the nose while you kick him in the butt', Co. 'A' took the Panthers under fire, losing three Shermans in the engagement that followed. In the meantime, Leach's company took advantage of the hills in the area to sweep against the laager's southern flank. They crested a ridge, guns blazing, quickly disabling several Panthers and forcing the survivors to flee under cover of dark and smoke grenades. The laager was overrun, littered with supplies and with the burning wrecks of nine Panthers.

A new M4A3E8 of the 25th Tank Bn., 14th Armd. Div. provides a clear view of the extent of sandbag armour additions. Indeed, the improvised armour covers so much of the hull front that the 14th Armd. Div. frequently painted the 'bumper' unit identification codes on the gun tube. The M4A3E8 was the culmination of Sherman tank development in the Second World War.

The Sherman in Allied Service

Besides the British and Commonwealth armoured units equipped with the Sherman, four other armies used the M4 series. French armoured units re-formed in North Africa in 1943 were equipped with the M4A2 Sherman. Three French divisions played a prominent role in the liberation of France: Gen. Leclerc's celebrated 2e Division Blindée, which landed at Normandy and was given the honour of liberating Paris, and the 1e and 5e Divisions Blindées, which took part in the invasion of southern France, fighting in the drive to the Swiss border and taking part in the tough battles in the Vosges. The Free Polish armoured units were also equipped with the M4 Sherman. The 1 Dywizja Pancerna, equipped with M4A4s, spearheaded the British and Canadian drive on

Falaise, bottling the Germans within the pocket. After suffering heavy casualties the division was re-equipped with M4A1(76mm) Ws and took part in the drive through the Low Countries, finishing the war with the capture of Wilhelmshaven. The 2 Brygada Pancerna, equipped with M4A2s, first went into action at Monte Cassino in 1944, took part in the liberation of Bologna, and in 1945 was enlarged to become the 2 'Warszawska' Dywizja Pancerna. The Soviet Army received 2,007 M4A2s with 75mm gun and 2095 M4A2(76mm) Ws, which were extensively used in the 1944 and 1945 campaigns in Central Europe. There were attempts to re-arm them with the F-34 76mm tank gun, resulting in the so-called M4M, but so much 75mm ammunition was provided through Lend-Lease that these modifications were not undertaken in any quantity. Although American military aid is played down in the Soviet Union, Soviet unit histories make it clear that American equipment was well liked. At least one of the Soviet tankers to win the coveted 'Hero of the Soviet Union' decoration, V. A. Galkin of the 7th Guards Cavalry Corp's 31st Tank Regiment, commanded an M4A2 Sherman. M4A4 Shermans of the American-trained 1st Chinese Provisional Tank Group fought in Burma in 1945.

A Soviet M4A2 tank crew brews up soup for supper in the early spring of 1945 on the Second Ukrainian Front in Czechoslovakia (Sovfoto)

The Sherman in Post-war Combat

After the war many Shermans were supplied to America's allies and, surprisingly, some remained in service into the early 1980s. In 1950 Shermans were recalled to duty during the Korean War, where the M4A3E8 proved quite successful in handling the T-34/85s of the North Korean 105th Armoured Brigade. They were eventually supplanted by M26 and M46 tanks, and the M4 gradually disappeared from US Army service in the 1950s. The Sherman played a prominent rôle in the four wars in the Middle East, 2 forming the backbone of the Israeli armoured force in 1947 and 1956, and serving in modified form in the 1967 and 1973 wars. The Egyptian Army also used the Sherman in 1947 and 1956. The Israelis supplied Shermans to Maj. Haddad's forces in southern Lebanon and to Phalangist militia in Beirut, where they have fought in the intractable Lebanese civil war.

Israeli-supplied Shermans also fought in the Ugandan Army during the downfall of Idi Amin, and in Nicaragua against the Sandanista rebels. The Battista regime in Cuba used Shermans against Castro's rebels, and these remained in service after Castro's takeover. At least one Castro Sherman fought against the M4Is landed during the abortive Bay of Pigs invasion. Shermans fought on both sides during the 1965 war in Kashmir between India and Pakistan. There were still about 40 in service with Pakistan in the 1971 war, serving with the 26th Cavalry at the battle for Chhamb. In the Far East, Shermans were used in modest numbers by the French in Indo-China, and by the Nationalist Chinese in the Civil War against Mao Tse-tung's forces.

THE PLATES

Plate A1: *M4A1, 2nd Platoon, 'G' Company, 1st Armored Regiment, US 1st Armored Division; Sidi-bou-Zid, Tunisia, February 1943*

This tank is finished in standard No. 9 Olive Drab, with an applied camouflage of greyish mud. In December 1942 the yellow star-and-bar Armored Force insignia reverted to white, as the yellow had a tendency to become obscured by dust. The diagonal bar and dot at the turret front indicates 'G' Co., 1st Regiment: the division used an elaborate system of geometrical markings to distinguish each company within the two regiments. The two dots further back indicate 2nd Platoon, and the '3' on the star is the vehicle number. The vehicle name, beginning with 'G', is obscured by the mud. A 20in. star was carried on the turret roof to the left, and a 60in. star on the engine deck, for air identification.

Plate A2: *M4A1, HQPltn., 'D' Co., 13th Tank Battalion, US 1st Armored Division; Italy, 1944*

This tank is finished in the FM-5-20B pattern of No. 9 Olive Drab with No. 8 Earth Red, and white undershading on the gun barrel and transmission housing. Most 1st Armd. Div. Shermans were left in overall Olive Drab, and this painting scheme was presumably the work of a camouflage engineer battalion. The division had an elaborate identification system for each platoon and company. Platoons were distinguished by barrelbands: one for 1st Pltn., two

A Soviet M4A2 Sherman tank crew celebrate VE day on top of their tank. This Sherman belonged to one of the brigades that met up with the US 82nd Airborne near Grabow, Germany. The slogan on the hull side reads 'Vpered k Pobyedye' – 'Forward to Victory!'.

for 2nd, three for 3rd, and four for HQ and FO tanks, and a half-band for command tanks. Originally these stripes were repeated on the rear turret sides as shown in the inset view, but subsequently a number was used instead. Platoon markings were painted in company colours, both the bands and the numbers. Under the old 'heavy' configuration with three companies per battalion the sequence was

red, white and blue. Under the 'light' configuration with four companies it changed to red for 'A', white for 'B', yellow for 'C', and blue for 'D' as here. Company commanders had a circular insignia with two horizontal bars (see inset view), platoon commanders a circle with one bar. The vehicle name is carried on the hull side. On the turret roof was a 20in. star, point forward, in a circular 4in. surround; a similar 60in. star was painted on the engine deck.

Plate B1: *M4 'Thunderbolt', command tank of Col. Creighton Abrams, 37th Tank Battalion, US 4th Armored Division; France, 1944*
The majority of 37th Bn. tanks had cartoons and names painted on the hull sides, 'Thunderbolt'

A tank of 'Rice's Red Devils', 'C' Co. of 89th Tank Bn., was one of the first across the Han River during the action in March 1951 near Uchonni, Korea This company, commanded by Capt. Clifford Rice, *painted red and white dragon faces on the fronts of their M4A3E8 Shermans in a curious attempt to intimidate the Chinese troops. One would imagine the 76mm gun would do a better job.*

A column of M4A4 Shermans of the Chinese 1st Provisional Tank Group in action in Burma in 1944. This unit was trained and raised with American support, and later fought in the Civil War against the Communists. Tiger faces were a popular decoration on the turrets of these vehicles.

being the insignia of Col. Abrams later US Army Chief of Staff during the Vietnam War, and after whom the new M1 tank is named. Aside from the usual star insignia on hull sides and turret roof, the regulation blue drab serial number is painted to the rear of the hull sides. On the rear deck is the fluorescent air identification panel. These came in two types, both 12ft. long by 3lins. wide: one was neon red (cerise) backed white, the other electric yellow backed white. The former was most commonly used by US armoured forces.

Plate B2: *M4, 3rd Pltn.,'B' Co., 8th Tank Battalion, US 4th Armored Division; Avranches, France, 1944*
The 8th was the most camouflage-conscious of the three battalions of the 4th Armored Division. After landing in Normandy they painted out all hull and turret stars, and welded iron rod to various points to allow the attachment of foliage. While several veterans insist that the tanks were not camouflage-painted, a number of photos clearly show a pattern of jagged blotches under the foliage, and these may have been applied with mud. They do not appear to have outlasted the August fighting. Some companies used platoon markings consisting of white bars on the rear hull sides and rear engine access door – one for 1st Pltn., two for 2nd, etc.

Plate C1: *M4A2, 2e Escadron, 12e Régiment de Chasseurs d'Afrique, 2e Division Blindée; France, summer 1944*
The French tank units raised with American aid

M4s of Israel's crack 7th Armoured Brigade parade in Tel Aviv in 1952. These Shermans were obtained through surreptitious channels in Europe, though later France supplied additional Shermans as the French Army began receiving more modern equipment. Israeli tank crews during this period wore Czechoslovak brown leather tankers' helmets of the Soviet variety. (IDF)

had an interesting and comprehensive set of markings to distinguish sub-units. The three tank regiments in each division bore a coloured square (blue in the 2^{e}DB, and probably green and red in the 1e and 5e DBs respectively) with the letter 'C' for 'char' tank and one to three bars. In the 2^{e}DB a bar across the top of the square indicated the 501e Régiment de Chars de Combat; one each side, the 12e Chasseurs d'Afrique; and one in all three positions, the 12e Cuirassiers. Small dashes added to one of these bars indicated the squadron within the regiment; thus the three inset views indicate, from left to right: 1^{er}Esc., 501^{e}RCC; 2^{e}Esc., 12^{e}RCA as marked on 'Tarentaise'; and 3^{e}Esc., 12^{e}RC. The tactical number on the turret indicated platoon and vehicle. Leclerc's 2^{e}DB used the blue and white map of France and Cross of Lorraine as a formation insignia, and tricolour national markings in several positions. The

12^{e}RCA had fought with the Free French in Tunisia in Somua S-35 tanks; when the unit traded its mounts the manufacturer's plate was in some cases removed from the Somuas and attached to the Shermans, out of sentiment. In front of the bow-gunner's position is taped a piece of paper with shipping data. A yellow and black British-style bridging class marking is painted at the front of the hull sides.

Plate C2: *M4A2, 3e Peleton, 4e Escadron, 2e Regiment de Cuirassicrs, 1e Division Blindée; Marseilles, 1944*

Since the 1^{e}DB did not use tactical turret numbers the platoons were identified in two other ways: small squares were painted on the regimental squadron insignia, and each platoon named its tanks beginning with a letter in rough alphabetical sequence. The platoon squares are shown in the three inset views: 1^{e}Pltn., 2^{e}Esc., senior regiment; 2^{e}Pltn., 4^{e}Esc., second senior regiment; and 3^{e}Pltn., 1^{er}Esc., third senior regiment. The initial letter of the name was painted large, and was repeated on the hull rear and sometimes to the rear of the turret sides. The squadron number was also painted on the hull rear. The 1^e and 5^{e}DBs used the same tricolour national marking with a white diamond centre; the 1^e positioned it horizontally, as here, and the 5^e, usually, in a vertical position, although a square presentation was sometimes seen on certain types of vehicle. The red and blue sections were occasionally painted out when on active service, leaving only the white diamond.

Plate D: *M4A4 Sherman with 75mm M3 gun and Chrysler A57 multibank engine*

The M4A4 Sherman shown here is typical of mid-war welded hull Sherman tanks. This particular variant was most commonly used by British and Commonwealth forces and is distinguished by its Chrysler multibank engine. Aside from the engine, and the lengthened hull it required, this variant is essentially similar to other Sherman tanks of this period. The crew configuration is very typical of World War II tanks. In the hull front are the driver on the left side, and a co-driver/machine gun operator on the right.

Between them is the vehicle's synchromesh transmission which drove the front-mounted drive sprockets. Front mounted transmissions meant that the power train to the engine had to go through the fighting compartment, under the turret basket, which was one reason for the relatively

high overall height of the Sherman compared to other World War II tanks such as the Russian T-34. The remaining three crewmen are in the turret: the tank commander and gunner in the right side of the turret and the loader in the left. The Sherman turret was fitted with a turret basket which made it easier for the turret crew to operate. Ready ammunition was stowed around the floor and sides of the turret basket, with other ammunition racks in the tank hull. The 75mm M3 gun as seen here was the standard M4 Sherman weapon until the summer of 1944 when the first 76mm gun Shermans saw their combat debut. Alongside the 75mm gun was a co-axial .30 calibre machine gun. The mid-war Shermans had only a

To extend the useful service life of the old Shermans the Israelis rebuilt many of them with new Cummins diesel engines, HVSS suspensions and new French 75mm high velocity tank guns. This M50 Super Sherman operating on the Golan Heights in 1970 is armed with the French SA50 gun which was derived from the 75mm gun in the Sherman's old adversary, the Panther. This view with the turret traversed to the rear clearly shows the large rear turret counter-weight extension needed to house this larger gun. (IDF)

single turret roof hatch which was inadequate in the event the vehicle was on fire. Later Shermans had an additional roof hatch added over the loader's station, as well as many other improvements.

Plate E1: M4A1(76mm)W, Lt. Tadeusz Wiatrowski, HQ Sqn. (Szwadron Dowodzenia), 2nd Armoured Regiment (2 Pulk Pancerny), 1st Polish Armoured Division (1 Dywizja Pancerna); Holland, 1944–45

'Latajaca Krowa' – 'Flying Cow' – was the personal insignia of the crew. The divisional insignia, a stylized 17th-century 'winged hussar' helmet, was carried at the front and rear of the hull, together with th standard British-pattern regimental tactical flash, in this case '52' in white on a red square.

The national flash, a white oval with a black 'PL' about 6ins. across, was normally marked on the hull rear at the centre or extreme left. The tank is finished in British Bronze Green, rather greener in shade than US Olive Drab. The gun barrel is painted at the end in lighter green and white, to make the length of the barrel less conspicuous to German AT gunners. This practice began in Normandy, when the 17pdr. Shermans were painted to resemble normal 75mm tanks during the battle of Falaise: the formidable Fireflies were naturally a

The ultimate Sherman must be the M51HV, a heavily modernised M4A1 armed with a 105mm gun designed in France. During the 1973 war these tanks held their own against modern Soviet tanks like the T-55. This was a remarkable tribute both to the durability of the basic Sherman design as well as to the skill of its crews.

priority target. The HQ Sqn. diamond is painted towards the rear of the hull sides. The presentation of the divisional insignia shown in the inset is somewhat more elaborate than that usually painted on the tanks.

Plate E2: M4A2, 2/Lt. Mieczyslaw Bialkiewicz, 2 Szwadron, 4 Pulk Pancerny, 2 Brygada Pancerna; Cassino, Italy, 1944

This Sherman was painted in the British 1943 scheme of Light Mud and Blue-Black while training in Palestine. The appliqué armour, added later, was Olive Drab. The tank name 'Pirat' was painted on the hull sides and rear. The Polish 4th Armoured Regiment took the nickname 'Skorpion' from its desert training; hence the turret insignia shown here. The inset views show the turret insignia of Shermans of the other armoured regiments of the brigade. The 1st Krechowiecki Lancers used a horse's head, and the 6th ('Children of Lwow') Armoured Regiment a rampant lion, taken from the city crest of Lwow. Subsequently, when the 2nd Polish Corps recce regiment – the Carpathian Lancers – received Shermans and joined the 2nd Armoured Division, they used an insignia reminiscent of the regimental collar badge: two palm trees rising from a crescent moon, all in white, superimposed on the regimental collar pennon, the whole enclosed by the squadron marking.

Plate F1: M4A1, 3rd Pltn., 'D' Co. of 66th or 67th Armored Regiment, US 2nd Armored Division; Cotentin Peninsula, France, August 1944

Tanks of the 2nd Armored Division originally had the company letter and platoon and tank numbers painted on each side of the turret star; but on arrival in France the star was painted out and the code simplified, as here. Eventually the turret numbers and letters were discontinued, as being too conspicuous. Here they are repeated on a sheet-metal rack added to the turret rear for stowage. At this stage the tanks were camouflaged by spraying swatches of No 5 Earth Brown over the base of No. 9 Olive Drab. The company letter and platoon and tank number are repeated on the differential housing in the normal manner. The official company

An M4A1(76mm, Remanufactured) lurks in hull defilade during the fighting in Kashmir. This vehicle, believed to be of the Pakistani 26th Cav. Regt., is armed with the 76mm M1 tank gun fitted in the older, smaller 75mm turret. During the 1965 war both the Pakistanis and the Indians used Sherman tanks, but the Pakistanis retained about 40 tanks like this one and used them again in the 1971 fighting. Unfortunately, by that late date they were hopelessly obsolete and suffered from numerous mechanical breakdowns. (Col. M. A. Durrani via George Balin)

initial name 'Derby' is supplemented by a cartoon of a child in a high chair and the slogan 'I Want You'. In front of this are stencilled shipping instructions, and a British-style bridge class marking.

Plate F2: M4A3E8, 781st Tank Battalion, US 100th Infantry Division; Bitche, France, March 1945

A good example of a heavily sandbagged tank. These modifications were frequently carried out by engineer companies, which finished the job off by repainting the whole vehicle, sandbags and all. In this case the Sherman is painted in the most common scheme – No. 10 Black sprayed over No. 9 Olive Drab.

Plate G1: M4A2 (76mm)W, Soviet 9th Guards Tank Brigade, 1st Guards Mechanised Corps; Budapest, Hungary, 1945

The 1st Guards Mechanised Corps was equipped entirely with Shermans. The tactical numbering system consisted of three digits, the first indicating the brigade: '1', '2', '3' and '9' identified respectively the 1st, 2nd and 3rd Guards Mechanised Brigades, and the 9th Guards Tank Brigade. The red hull slogan is 'Za Rodinu!' 'For the Homeland!'

Plate G2: *M4A2(76mm)W, unidentified Soviet tank brigade; Berlin, 1945*

Finished in overall No. 9 Olive Drab, this tank carries a geometric tactical insignia which presumably identified its brigade within its corps. The white band and roof cross were adopted by Soviet tanks in April 1945 to identify them to prowling Allied aircraft. The Soviets originally suggested that their tanks carry one turret stripe and British and American tanks two stripes, but the US Army was satisfied with its fluorescent identification panels. In May 1945 the Soviet marking was changed to turret triangles after German Panzer crews started painting roof crosses on their tanks, having discovered their significance.

INDEX

(References to illustrations are shown in **bold**. Plates are shown with page and caption locators in brackets.)